Trump vs America

A Grand Conspiracy to Bring Down a World Power

TABLE OF CONTENTS

Contents

The United States of America has been the most powerful nation in the world for decades. Repeated challenges have only made it stronger. Its power lies in its ability to unite its citizens around their love of country.

But the story of our nation has always been a turbulent one. How then, is the current crisis in our nation, occasioned by the ascension to the Presidency of a businessman unschooled in the ways of government, threatening to pull it apart at the very seams?

The terror attack of September 11, 2001 gave rise to an era in which Americans were sharply divided along ideological lines, but there have been numerous other periods in history which had a similar effect, including the Civil War and the Civil Rights Era. How did we pull together as a nation in the wake of these events and how can we achieve that, once again?

The grand conspiracy we face in the USA today is the work of forces external to this nation and its government. There is abundant evidence to suggest that the Russian Federation is at the center of it.   The investigation into this conspiracy posits that the President, himself, is the Trojan horse, by which America may be compelled to fall, due to the implication of numerous of his aides and associates in what may well have been a fraudulent and invalid presidential election.

But how do we, as Americans respond? How do we once again pull together in common cause to answer this existential threat, igniting again the unquenchable flame of our nation? This book is dedicated to these questions.

INTRODUCTION

All over the world, when you pronounce the letters "USA", people respond with enthusiasm. That enthusiastic response can be anything from contempt to adoration. When you're as big and bold as the USA, opinions are bound to be strong.

That's something everyone reading this is knows.

But what makes us the United States of America? Is it our very unique political culture and system of governance? Is it the mosaic of our diversity, as a people? Perhaps it's in the fabric of our democracy and our stated dedication to freedom that we find the true meaning of our community of semi-autonomous states - a union which can always be made more perfect.

But in 2017, we face an existential crisis as a nation. It's not the first challenge, by any means. Throughout its existence, the United States has met numerous challenges, from the Civil War to the Era of Civil Rights, to that terrifying day in 2001 when we were attacked by terrorists in our most iconic city.

This one is different. Since his election as President on November 8, 2016, Donald J. Trump has been a deeply divisive figure. The election itself reflects the divided nature of public opinion, with the numbers revealing a sharply ideological split which runs right through the heart of the United States.

Those who love Donald Trump are immovable in their devotion, but their numbers hover at less than 1/3rd of Americans. Slowly, his base is eroding as his repeatedly stated intention to "Make America Great Again" is increasingly seen as an empty slogan.

For those of us who love this country, it's clear that America was already great. There is no question that we have been largely a force for good in a world desperately in need of a steady hand. But the slogan is resilient. It is as impervious to reasoned examination as it is empty.

Now, with revelations of interference by the Russian Federation in the presidential elections, the very fabric of our beloved democracy appears to have been rent asunder. As Americans look on in horror, revelations of Russian trolls and hackers deliberately targeting American voters (and in the instances of three states, vote counts) grow in significance.

Our identity as a beacon of democracy, justice and freedom is at stake. As we consider the possibility that our cherished democracy has been abused and manipulated by a hostile foreign power, neighbor turns against neighbor, looking for someone to blame.

And that's the question on my mind, as I write. Who is to blame for all this?

This book will examine some of the most compelling possibilities and arrive at a solution to our current turmoil, rooted in the rule of law and our ultimate responsibility as citizens of this nation we all love.

CHAPTER ONE

AN UNQUENCHABLE FLAME

While the subject of this book is not the history of the USA, some key moments in our history will reveal that our nation has always had the ability to recover from difficult, even catastrophic, events.

Born in the crucible of people fleeing the tyranny of the British Crown, the USA began as an experiment. Could people from the Old World establish themselves in this unknown continent, with its vastness; its seemingly limitless vistas?

But early settlers knew that it was not just the size of the land they were putting down stakes in that appeared limitless. It was also the potential of that land and its promise.

Based on the premise that it's hard to know where you're going when you don't know where you've been, I've selected some pivotal moments from our history which I believe to be both formative and demonstrative of our resilience as a nation. But these moments are also instructive, in that they demonstrate the ability of our nation to build something of great value in what appear to be hopeless ruins.

All are moments of turmoil and triumph, revealing an unquenchable flame that sometimes burns out of control, burning us all, as it does so. Yet, this is the same flame which illuminates the heart of every living American. We may not always see things the same way, but like the Olympic torch bearers, the flame in our hearts is from a single source – in our case, love of country.

Colonies in conflict

The United States was wrought in turmoil, occasioned by a series of events which led to the British Crown issuing what were known as the Intolerable Acts. Precipitating the passage of this legislation was what we today call the Boston Tea Party. A large shipment of tea was dumped from a ship by Patriot colonists in protest of changes to taxation.

Massachusetts, under this legislation, lost its right to self-governance. This sparked outrage in the Thirteen Colonies of the day, which in turn led to the American Revolution, which began in 1775.

It was on July 4, 1776 that the Declaration of Independence was approved at the Second Continental Congress, officially codifying the birth of a new reality – a United States of America, fully independent of British rule. It was not until 1782, as battles with British Loyalists raged across the nascent USA, that the British government would officially (while not formally) recognize US independence.

In September of 1783, the Treaty of Paris ended the American Revolutionary War.

But there was to be no peace in the new nation, as it struggled against enemies both outside and within its borders. Unrest and struggle are the lot of any new nation, as factions coalesce around their desired visions of what that nation is to be. But for the young USA, the road to peace would be arduous and long.

A formative document

In 1823, President James Monroe created the policy which would form the basis of US foreign policy into the 20th Century. The last President to invoke its tenets as a foreign policy imperative was Ronald Reagan. Originally intended to protect the USA from interference by European powers, the Monroe Doctrine (a moniker it was graced with in 1850) continues to influence the spirit of US foreign policy.

The Monroe Doctrine acted a support for galvanizing stewardship of the Americas (as a whole) on the part of the USA, defining the USA and the nations of the Americas as the New World. Europe was the Old World and the policy established a cordon located somewhere in the Atlantic Ocean that the Old World was not to breach.

The theory at work was that there would be no more colonies established in the Americas, as the nations of Latin America were rapidly gaining independence from the European powers previously governing their affairs. In practice, the Monroe Doctrine established a "sphere of influence" for the USA and was the basis for its own expansionist ambitions in the Americas.

As the USA grew, the Monroe Doctrine assisted it in becoming a world power. This is the cornerstone of the USA's international influence and power. In sum, the Monroe Doctrine established the USA's turf and put the Old World on notice that there was a new sheriff in town.

Meanwhile, back home, the USA dealt with internal challenges to government power, including those emanating from Native American communities. This challenge was met with legislation which mandated the removal of these communities from land desired for settlement and early development.

As the West was being forged and the great cities of the nation formed from coast to coast, the turmoil continued, keeping pace with the growth of the international power.

The Mexican-American War

Following the annexation of Texas by the USA in 1845, the United Mexican States went to war with the USA. They had considered Texas to be a northern province, despite the Texas Revolution of 1836.

The war raged for two years, until the Treaty of Guadalupe Hidalgo ended the war in 1848. But this détente came at great cost to Mexico. It not only lost Texas, but all the territories to the west, extending north to Oregon. Its northern border was re-established as the Rio Grande.

Mexico lost fully 1/3 of its territories in the war, while the USA suddenly resembled the nation we know today, in terms of size, shape and land mass. This had been President James R. Polk's fondest dream, as his vision was of an America which stretched from sea to shining sea. He had even offered to purchase some of the territories gained in the treaty, but Mexico had refused.

His answer? War.

The Civil War

There has been much debate about the Civil War and its causes, but it's simply undeniable that the institution of slavery and the intransigence of the southern states in confrontation of proposed abolition was the root cause.

Slavery was primarily an economic construct. It allowed the plantation culture of the region to flourish, based as it was on unpaid labor. But slavery went well beyond that. To attain that unpaid labor, brutality was required to ensure the workforce remained in place and subject to rule by plantation owners and their operations.

In 1860, South Carolina seceded from the Union of States. The following year, 10 more southern states followed, forming the Confederate States of America. In these actions lie the seeds of the USA's current turmoil.

The United States and its flag continues to be challenged by forces which have yet to accept that the Confederacy lost the war (with many continuing to refer to it as the War of Northern Aggression). Confederate flags, while disappearing from government buildings in many jurisdictions, continue to be proudly displayed by this faction and carried in demonstrations. The defenders of this flag, itself a challenge to the unity of the USA claim it as "heritage."

The Civil War represents an enormous wound on the American psyche. It's a wound which, as discussed above, has never truly healed. It continues to ooze, producing intermittent waves of pain which wash over the nation with disturbing regularity.

From 1861 to 1865, American citizens took up arms against one another. What precipitated this conflict? Simply, the Confederacy litigated for States' Rights to uphold and expand the institution of slavery. The battle had been brewing for years, with various accommodations and skirmishes occurring between abolitionists and the advocates of slavery.

Between 620,000 and 750,000 Americans died in the conflict. These figures represent more combined deaths in the theater of war than all other military conflicts the USA has ever been involved in – combined.

This staggering human cost was accompanied by economic collapse in the South, with infrastructure destroyed and 4 million slaves freed, as slavery was abolished at the close of the war.

Followed by Reconstruction (1863-1877), during which freed slaves were given civil rights and national unity was restored, the American Civil War is the grievous cut in the body politic which continues to bleed. Its wounds have never fully healed. The fact that Confederate flags continue to fly in various parts of the nation bears witness to this horrible truth.

The assassination of Abraham Lincoln in April 15, 1865, immediately after the surrender of

General Lee to Union forces, made him the war's final casualty.

Or did it? The Civil War continues to haunt the USA in symbolism, threats of secession by a variety of states and the removal of monuments erected in sympathy to the Confederacy, long after the War was over. Its reverberations can be felt today, in the continuing presence of militia organizations and the demonstrations in Charlottesville (where a woman was killed when a white supremacist drove into her) and other cities, across the country.

The shadow of those four turbulent years still stretches across the length and breadth of our great nation. It was, in fact, the echoes of the Civil War which gave birth to another turbulent period in our history – the Civil Rights Era.

Civil Rights Era (1955-1968)

The Civil War pitted American against American. The contentious issue of states' rights to mandate slavery as an acceptable institution was the cause. There is no question. Neither is there any question that it's in the fallout from that war that we find the origins of the Civil Rights Era.

Reconstruction efforts after the Civil War sought to address the civil rights of freed slaves. But the application of legislation, in regions hostile to the very idea of freed slaves, proved difficult, if not impossible.

Public resistance to the advent of freed Blacks gave rise to movements to again strip them of their rights, culminating in a variety of laws which made life as a freed slave hellish. As free people of color attempted to take the rights which had been granted them, the supporters of the lost cause and those who could not countenance the competition represented by 4 million more people in the workforce, pushed back.

Homer Plessy's attempt to board a whites-only trolley car in New Orleans (an act which resulted in the institution of the Separate but Equal law in 1896, at the end of the Plessy vs. Ferguson case) was a foundational moment which changed the way Blacks felt about the way they were being treated as free people.

There were two distinct movements in American history which addressed the rights of Blacks, prior to one which began in 1955. These spanned the years 1865-1896 and 1896-

1954. Those who believe that the Civil Rights Era was in any way an isolated effort led by only one small faction of people, from 1955-1968, should know that the work of gaining civil rights endured for over 100 years of fully engaged struggle.

Emmett Till murder, 1955

In 1955, a 14-year-old boy travelled from Chicago, Illinois to Money, Mississippi to visit relatives living there. Having been raised in a city with considerably less Black/White tension than existed in Mississippi at the time, Emmett Till walked into a cauldron of hatred.

Accused of wolf-whistling a local shopkeeper's wife (a claim she retracted many years later), Emmett Till was kidnapped by two local men (one of whom was the shopkeeper). He was tortured, mutilated (one of his eyes was gouged out) and murdered, his body thrown in the Tallahatchie River.

Three days later, his body was found. The event, in the age of television, would gain national attention, in turn drawing the nation's gaze toward the injustice of the Jim Crow Laws. This is widely viewed as the genesis of the Civil Rights Movement of the 1950s and 1960s, a movement which would see enormous change for people of color across the nation.

Jim Crow

The Jim Crow laws were enacted as a means of segregating Blacks from Whites. This collection of laws was enacted across the Southern States, at the state and municipal level, following the Reconstruction Period and enduring until the mid-1960s. These laws revived the previous Black Codes of 1865 and 1866, which were used to curtail the rights of Black Americans

The name "Jim Crow" is a derogatory description of Black Americans, derived from a character popularized by a white minstrel performer, Thomas Dartmouth Rice, who performed in black face.

Rice based his character on a folkloric personality in Black slave culture, named Jim Crow, after whom the Rice's popular song, Jump Jim Crow, was named.

And so, a character born from the institution of slavery became a symbol of the repression of Black presence in public spaces, including transit, schools, lunch counters and other areas. The Jim Crow laws were subject to interpretation and many whites felt it was their duty to interpret them both strictly and liberally.

That meant Blacks were to avert their eyes in the presence of white people and walk with their heads down in the streets, never making eye contact. It was even considered a legal challenge not to yield the sidewalk to white pedestrians, if you lived under these laws and were Black.

But the Jim Crow laws were to slowly fall to successive legal challenges, beginning with Brown vs. Board of Education in 1954, which deemed segregation in schools unconstitutional. Ten years later, the Civil Rights Act (1964) and the Voting Rights Act (1965) would ostensibly end the tyranny of these laws, by codifying the civil rights of Black Americans at the federal level. The Fair Housing Act would come in 1968. It's said that the price of that legislation was the blood of the leader of the movement, Dr. Martin Luther King Jr., who was assassinated on the balcony of his Memphis hotel on April 4, 1968.

The Civil Rights Era was a formative moment in the story of the USA. The great victories it's responsible for, however, continue to be fought on the streets of American cities, as young Black men and women are repeatedly singled out, profiled, abused and even murdered by police.

Emmett Till's murder set in motion the seismic shift represented by the Civil Rights Era, yet his shadow still falls across America, in names like Oscar Grant and Sandra Bland.

In 2016, unarmed Black men between the ages of 15-34 were 9 times more likely than any other American demographic to be shot dead by police.

911

As with the shocking assassination of John F. Kennedy in 1963, everyone in the USA remembers clearly where they were, when they first heard that our nation was under terrorist attack in both Washington, DC and New York City.

As for the author, I was on my honeymoon. I awoke to a call from a friend telling me to turn on the television. What I saw and what we all saw, defied belief. The Pentagon and the World Trade Center had been attacked and while I watched, the second tower was hit by an airplane.

While this incident threw the United States into a state of extreme turmoil, rendering us by turns angry, frustrated and lashing out at the world, it also turned us against it each other. 911 changed the world forever. It tore at the fabric our country, but also of the world. We knew, in that moment, that nothing would ever be the same.

And many of us knew exactly where we stood and that our stance was immutable. It's the very resolve and independence of thought associated with being American that set us against one other, with voices rising in protest over the planned response to the attack.

Propelled into the theater of war with lightning speed, Americans looked on in horror as embedded reporters bellowed from tanks as they raced through the desert, headed for Baghdad and the redress of wrongs (even though the 911 terrorists were mostly Saudi Arabian. Fifteen of the 19 involved were Saudi, with the balance being from Egypt, the United Arab Emirates and Lebanon).

In 911, the American tradition of public dissent found a Waterloo. Those against the Iraq were branded traitors. Sharp divides appeared in families, marriages, between co-workers and lifelong friends.

Those who supported the war demanded retribution. Those who opposed it, wondered why we were attacking Iraq, when not one of the terrorists involved in 911 originated from that nation.

United we stand

I've selected the foregoing historical episodes, because I believe each one of them tells an important story about who we are as a nation. Each of these historical vignettes is instructive and those in which our divisions have been most stark have the power to instruct us today, as we face the distinct possibility that our own President is beholden to a foreign power.

After the Civil War, even focused Reconstruction could not prevent the rise of laws intended to appease the resentment felt in the South. That resentment coalesced around the public presence of Americans who had been brought to our shores as slaves and were now free. Jim Crow came and once again, we were divided from one another.

Still, though, the unquenchable flame which animates our great nation has continued to burn.   Through wars between brothers, divisions chosen because of skin color and historical grudges and through ideological disagreements about who to go to war with, it yet burns.

But that flame is not the "rocket's red glare". It's in the heart of every American. We may be 50 states, but we are more. We may be fractious and turbulent, but we rise above. In every moment of our nation's serial struggles and triumphs, we have found it in ourselves to unite behind our shared love for the USA.

And yet, the cauldron continues to bubble. Now that it's coming to a boil, it's time for us to do some serious soul-searching and to interrogate what this new presidency and the administration it governs really means to the future of this great nation.

CHAPTER TWO

E PLURIBUS UNUM

Until 1956, when the House of Representatives adopted our national motto, "In God we Trust." This was our nation's mission statement. Formulated in 1782, "E Pluribus Unum" came into being via the same legislative body it was later changed by.

The USA's mission as a nation was to create from the diversity of its people and territories, one reality. Joining in unity, American citizens were to be held together in devotion to the idea of America, regardless of any other identity.

The motto appears to this day on the Great Seal, inscribed on the banner grasped by our national symbol, the Bald Eagle.

And yet, unity continues to be an elusive reality in the United States. The presidential election of 2016 tells the tale of nation sharply divided along ideological lines. We live in camps of thinking delineated not just by the left and right of the political spectrum, but by ethnic identity.

Our growing alienation

Pew Research reports that our divisions are only growing deeper. The deeper the cut, the more difficult it is to heal. Over the past 60 years, what it means to support the person of the President has changed dramatically.

Americans are now much less likely to support a President who doesn't reflect their ideological worldview. And this is not merely a matter of party politics. It goes deeper than that. Americans on both sides of the political divide want a leader who adheres to the values they do, personally.

We are no longer content with competencies. We want to see our values reflected in each minute detail, including whether the President is pro-choice, or anti, a church-going Christian who loves guns, or a confirmed pacifist who wants to Make America Great Again through the fine art of diplomacy. We want to see someone in office who makes sense to us and aligns with the values we believe are the right ones, because we believe them to be distinctively American.

As a nation, we have come to the point where we squat in opposite sides of the room, waiting for the opposition to admit it's wrong. But as political realities become increasingly entrenched, people dig in their heels.

We all need to be right so desperately, that we're willing to wait – for two planes to smash into buildings in a major city, or a conveniently unifying war. Or maybe what we want is someone to believe in – someone who will Make America Great Again by sheer force of his iron will.

We seek a savior from ourselves who will swoop down like our national symbol, the mighty Bald Eagle and salve that great wound which will not heal.

Numbers don't lie

A look at the distribution of the popular vote in the 2016 presidential election is revealing. With the current President taking 46.1% and the Democrat challenger taking 48.2%, it's obvious that both candidates inspired strong feelings.

But ultimately, the Electoral College decides the fate of presidential candidates and thus, Donald J. Trump was declared the winner. Despite having a slightly lower percentage of the popular vote, he received the requisite Electoral College votes required – the deciding factor.

Numbers are instructive. They have no passions, or interests. They illuminate a nation divided along lines which are demographic, with ideologies adhering to the demographic markers involved.

For example, white voters turned out for Trump in droves. His share of the white vote was 58%, against his opponent's 37%. Among Black voters, Democratic Party challenger, Hillary Clinton, won by 88%, against Trump's 8%.

This alone tells us something we probably don't want to hear. Can it be that the advent of a Black President in Barack Obama was received by White America as a threat to its existence? The White House has never hosted a President who was not white.

Nor has it hosted a President who was not male.

And so, the very thought of a woman following a Black man into the White House stirred ancient grudges and hostilities previously believed buried, by all but the few who have been paying close attention.

54% of white women voted for Trump. There is a sense of tribal loyalty in this statistic which can't be ignored. When faced with a white female candidate, white women were unmoved by her sex. They voted for the white male.

Education levels were another telling statistic in the 2016 election. Voters without college degrees voted overwhelmingly for Trump, breaking for him at a rate of 52% to Clinton's 44%. This statistic is even higher among whites without a college degree. Fully 67% of them voted for Trump. This represents the greatest percentage of this group voting for a single candidate in any election since 1980.

What these numbers are telling us (and not at all subtly) is that the USA's ancient resentments are closer to the surface than they have been for over half a century. The Obama effect cannot be denied.

Diversity as threat
While many Americans take pride in the great melting pot the United States is known as, others view diversity as an existential threat.

The more of "them" there are, it seems, the more some of us take the defensive stance.

The global economic collapse of 2008 took from many Americans what we've always considered our birthright – our prosperity, our homes, our savings and our sense of security. Personal fortunes gained over lifetimes were lost and the injustice of it all was most baldly seen in the bank bailout.

As Americans watched from their life rafts, the great Titanic of banking slipped under the dark waters and was engulfed by chaos. But in the 11th hour, our government swooped down and George Walker Bush signed TARP (Troubled Asset Relief Program) into law.

The banks could not fail. They were just too big to allow that to happen and so, after pushing the world economy to brink of disaster, the government threw a great deal of money at them.

It stuck its finger in the dam to the tune of $700 billion.

The ripples of the great ship of banking disappearing under the waters were to be felt for years. It's only recently that optimism has been restored – but not in all quarters.

The election of Barack Obama coincided with the devastation of 2008, combined with the effects of two prolonged wars in Iraq and Afghanistan and the financial demands made of the treasury by these conflicts. Americans were still reeling from 911 and the ripples of the Titanic economic collapse when the first Black President came long, grinning from ear to ear.

"Yes, we can!" he said.

This rallying cry was to be a call for civic engagement on the part of all Americans, variously taken up. Barack Obama's intent was to bring together the diverse elements of the USA, from the hardworking immigrants from south of the border, to the forgotten workers of America's manufacturing centers, waiting for someone to care. From Detroit's auto workers, to fast food and retail employees, working for a minimum wage that didn't even pay their bills, Obama demanded that Americans behave like Americans. He had a vision of pulling us all together in the great project of rebuilding from the former devastations of terrorist acts, economic catastrophe and perpetual war.

He called all Americans – not just those who looked like him or thought like him. He called the Black, the white and the immigrant. The Christian, the Jew and the Muslim. He called to the unquenchable flame in the heart of every American to Make America Great Again, after all it had endured.

And he enjoyed such success in doing so that he served two scandal-free terms, emerging on the other side of what he'd done bloodied, but unbowed. But his presidency was not the love fest he had hoped for.

He believed that America was "post-racial", an assertion floated at his acceptance speech in Grant Park, Chicago, before an audience of millions, all over the world.

About this, Obama was profoundly mistaken. His optimism had gotten the better of him.

Obama derangement syndrome

Obama's optimism, while a decisive factor in both his election to the Office of President and his subsequent re-election to a second term, was an Achilles' heel. He entered office with a belief in the goodness of the American people.

But, over time, he was to find that the goodness he believed in was unevenly distributed. Even before his election, he was repeatedly assaulted by the assertion that he hadn't even been born in the USA, but in Kenya, in Africa. This prompted President Obama, on June 12, 2008, to release his short form birth certificate (certification of live birth, from the State of Hawaii).

But conspiracy theories continued to swirl. Although many believed the matter to be summarily closed, some wanted it resurrected and one voice in the effort was persistent.

That of Donald J. Trump.

In 2011 (the year before his first run to gain the Republican Party's endorsement as candidate for the presidency), now-President Donald Trump began to hint at the idea that Obama had not been born in the USA. While evidence of his birth had already been made available, Trump's demand for evidence of both the President's birthplace (he demanded a long form certificate) and his achievements at Harvard University, continued.

In 2012, Trump tweeted that he had it from reliable sources that the short form certificate released in 2008 was a "fraud." Then, in 2014, he called on internet hackers to obtain Obama's college records to check them for his place of birth, suggesting that they'd been destroyed.

Finally, in September of 2016, only weeks before the presidential election, Trump conceded that President Obama had, indeed, been born in the USA. He then blamed Democratic Party candidate Clinton for the entire sordid affair.

Not only did Trump revive the dead theory of Obama's foreign birth, throwing into question the then-President's honesty and validity as a President. He attempted to pin that revival on his opponent, after cultivating the conspiracy theory for five long years, actively and deliberately.

Seen from the other side of history, the Birther narrative is not just unfortunate. It reflected the ancient hostility of the Civil War rather baldly. Never before, in the history of the presidency, has such scrutiny been applied to the birthplace of a candidate. But this candidate was different.

This candidate was Black.

Throughout his presidency, Barack Obama was to be hanged in effigy, depicted as a watermelon chomping caricature and serially insulted by those who could not accept the advent of a Black President. Obama Derangement Syndrome is entirely sited in his ethnicity. It was not driven by GOP-supporting voters' disappointment over a lost election. It was driven by the same hostilities which led the USA into a war against itself and those which had ignited the conflagration in the South, in the form of the Jim Crow laws.

It was these same hostilities which were to coalesce around a GOP candidate who promised to Make America Great Again (even though this effect had already been achieved). The MAGA slogan signaled a restoration of order in the minds of Trump's supporters and that order was resolutely and exclusively Caucasian.

CHAPTER THREE

ANGRY, RESENTFUL, SMUG AND CLUELESS

"The Trump Administration has managed to highlight the two least attractive aspects of American conservatism: an angry and resentful populism, and a smug and clueless plutocracy. It's an impressive feat."

-- Republican pundit William Kristol

Today editor of the conservative publication, The Weekly Standard, William Kristol is a longtime Republican Party operative and commentator. Arriving in Washington, DC in 1976, as campaign manager for the Senatorial run of Democratic Party candidate Daniel Patrick Moynihan, Kristol was later to cleave to the GOP to become a major voice for its policies and imperatives.

Kristol stands as a symbol of the sharp rift caused in the Republican Party by candidate and now-President Trump. The quote shown above reveals the depths of that rift and the shift in the concept of "conservatism" in recent decades.

Conservatism, in the world of American politics, no longer means "to struggle for the continuation of institutions and policies which best reflect values of moderation and fiscal prudence". Conservatism now means a type of extremism which is anathema to earlier incarnations of the GOP.

The "angry and resentful populism" to which Kristol refers in the quote is nothing new. It's always been lurking just beneath the surface of the public square, threatening to break through the common decency of the American democratic model, spewing forth with the natural force of Old Faithful.

The "smug and clueless plutocracy" referred to is inherent to the current administration. As the President's approval numbers dip lower than any US President's since the institution of public polls were introduced (38.3%, against a disapproval rating of 57.3% at the 300-day mark), this presenting feature has become increasingly apparent.

Before we go on, let's define a couple of terms.

Populism

The presidential election of 2018 was uniquely marked by populism. Harnessing the resentment of a targeted demographic, populism seeks to satisfy the simmering hostilities of those who feel they've been overlooked. Gathering them under the tent of dissatisfaction and anger, populism identifies a source for the woes of its audience and then uses them to mobilize emotions, framing them as policy.

On the left, Bernie Sanders ran a campaign entirely built on the resentments of young people and leftists, mobilizing those resentments against the rich and powerful. Promising sweeping change which would transform the fortunes of these factions, Sanders directed his fiery declamations at "the 1%" and the presumptive nominee, Clinton. By identifying Clinton as a water bearer for the wealthy elites and a person of dubious character, he set the stage for soon-to-be President Trump's own campaign cry of "Crooked Hillary."

On the right, Trump's campaign framed the billionaire businessman as an "everyman". In the style of the film *Face in the Crowd,* he appealed to the sentiments of those he was reaching out to. Using simple to understand words and slogans, he directly targeted a disaffected sector, frustrated by change. But Trump was no Lonesome Rhodes hayseed, suddenly catapulted to power and fortune.

Trump was already there. And in the minds of his followers, that made him even more attractive.

By drawing on the resentments of his supporters (mostly ethnically-based), Trump promised to build a wall to keep out the Mexicans who were stealing American jobs. Typifying Mexicans as "rapists and criminals," he took up a populist narrative which energized his target demographic. Identifying the source of his followers' woes, siting them in immigrant Mexicans, Muslims, "thugs" (a dog whistle term indicating "Black") and of course, Obama, Trump created a cauldron of simmering hatreds, bringing it to the forefront and legitimizing it.

He re-created himself as a sympathetic champion, come to salve the wounds of White America. By modelling speech and behavior outside the bounds of accepted norms of societal decorum, he became the champion of saying whatever pops into your head, regardless of who it wounds – include many Americans.

Untethered to political correctness, he was giving his followers permission to behave in the same manner. He was giving them free rein to break with common decency and cut loose.

Plutocracy

When the American President is a symbol of ultimate wealth (even though the state of his fortunes continues to be veiled in mystery and obfuscation), plutocracy is bound to arise.

Referring to the exclusive rule, whether by law or by other means, of a wealthy ruling class, plutocracy puts the reins of power into the hands of any given jurisdiction's wealthiest members.

The Secretary of State, Rex Tillerson, comes to us from the oil industry, as former CEO of ExxonMobil. The Secretary of Education, Betsey De Vos, is a member of an extraordinarily wealth family and a billionaire herself. Her family fortunes were made through sales under the Amway banner, which many have described as a pyramid scheme with a friendly face.

The President's Cabinet is worth no less than $14 billion, collectively, compromising of millionaires and billionaires exclusively.

While promising to "drain the swamp" (as Benito Mussolini also promised in pre-WWII Italy), the President's Cabinet selections reveal the promise as the empty slogan it is. Whether qualified for their positions or not, members of Trump's Cabinet are also members of the wealthy elite which characterize plutocratic rule.

As the hopeful coal worker looks on from the heartland, America's new government tailors its policies to the desires of those positioned to benefit most handsomely from the newly-approved tax policy, adopted recently in Congress. With access to every tentacle of government, America's wealthy stand to benefit even further, by diminishing the ability of average struggling Americans to move forward in their lives.

By instituting policies which benefit themselves and their peers first, the idea of America is subsumed. And all this is courtesy of the populism so deftly employed to harness the simmering rage of Trump's most ardent supporters.

When populism meets plutocracy

Populism is rarely in the service of the common good. Rarely uniting, it is division's most potent weapon.

Just as Bernie Sanders drew lines across the face of America, dividing it in terms of class and economic status, Donald Trump drew stark lines which divided it in terms of ethnicity, sex and religion.

Populism is the engine of plutocracy. By telling a distinct group what it wanted to hear, Donald Trump was able to achieve a sparse government infrastructure (hundreds of key positions remain unfilled in Washington, to this day), consolidating power around a cabinet consisting of the wealthy and forwarding their interests.

The upturned faces at a Trump rally reveal a constituency desperate to be recognized.

Illuminated by the golden calf before it, all that glitters is presumed to be gold. Every word is gospel. Every gesture, intensely followed.

As most of us observed the phenomenon of the Trump Train which rolled across the USA's expanses in 2016, we saw in it no liberation from a deficit of greatness. We saw in it a profound danger. We saw the divisions being actively fostered and legitimized. Ethnic hatreds were suddenly being spoken out loud from the podium of a presidential candidate.

Protestors (seeing what most of us did in this candidate's comportment) at Trump rallies were repeatedly attacked with aggression and violence, with the candidate encouraging his acolytes from the podium. On more than occasion, candidate Trump offered to pay the legal fees of supporters who attacked and injured protestors.

Of one protestor in Michigan, he said, "I'd like to punch the hell out of him," as the objecting party was led away by security.

These eruptions of violence by Trump supporters at rallies continued apace throughout the campaign. A suit was eventually brought by three protestors who were attacked at a rally, one of them sucker-punched by a Trump supporter.

Initially dismissed, on March 31 of this year, Judge David J. Hale, a Federal Justice in Kentucky, ruled that the charges would not be dismissed, but heard. The suit alleges that the candidate actively encouraged the violence alleged in the suit from the podium.

Judge Hale has expressly refused to dismiss this charge, due to repeated violent eruptions at Trump rallies, which the candidate either encouraged, or failed to vigorously discourage.

Trump had ordered the removal of the three protestors, prompting the violence. The case has now been referred to Magistrate Judge H. Brent Brennenstuhl.

As the engine of plutocracy, populism seeks to assure a targeted constituency that they have been egregiously wronged by an "other"; an interloper responsible for the perceived wrongs suffered.

In Trump's case, the brush was broad, encompassing identifiable "enemies of the people" in the media (particularly media which was not supportive of his candidacy) and other groups, mostly delineated by either ethnicity or religion.

MAGA

The defining slogan of Trump's campaign was Make America Great Again.

Implicit in the slogan is the concept that America was "not great"; that it had been degraded from its former status by forces which sought its destruction. The MAGA slogan, at its heart, is an insult to the USA and the people who live in it, but not all received it that way. Supporters of Trump were being told exactly what they wanted to hear – that the country had gone to hell in a handbasket.

And while he was telling them that, he was telling them why this happened and who was responsible. In doing so, he brought the hostility of White America (at least that portion of it which perceived to have lost traction in the socio-political environment which has prevailed in recent decades).

At his rallies, Trump painted a dystopian picture of the USA. Its factories were deserted. Its urban areas were riddled with crime and murder. Its borders were dangerously porous, allowing "rapists and criminals" to seep in through its pores like toxic, corrosive elements.

He proposed as part of his project to Make America Great Again, that the USA build a wall at its border with Mexico to contain the threat represented by that nation's people.

"I will build a great wall — and nobody builds walls better than me, believe me —and I'll build them very inexpensively. I will build a great, great wall on our southern border, and I will make Mexico pay for that wall. Mark my words."

- **Donald J. Trump**

Mexico was, without doubt, very surprised to hear that it would now be paying for something it had not commissioned.

This quote, from June 2015, is the very first mention of Trump's fabled wall, but he would ramp up the Wall rhetoric, as the campaign went on, because the thought of being walled in against the vast tide of unwelcome brown people appealed enormously to the constituency being targeted by his baldly race-baiting narrative.

In fact, the Wall narrative would be distilled into a chant, for use at his rallies to further inflame his already restive supporters. "Build that wall!" became the battle cry of Trump Nation.

But the problem with giant border walls, 30-feet high and running the length of the continent is that they are expensive. Trump's original estimate for construction was $12 billion. But that figure was revealed to be optimistic by a report released in February 2017 by the Department of Homeland Security. The leaked report's figure was $21.6 billion, causing Congressional Republicans to bridle at the price tag.

Regardless of his claims to the contrary, candidate Trump knew it was going to be costly. He also knew that Mexico would not be accepting his kind invitation to pay for the wall.

And so, in January of 2017, he walked back his earlier claim that Mexico would pay for his Great Wall of Trump, saying that our neighbor to the south would pay "at some time in the future", via a tax created for that purpose or a direct payment. His reasoning? That he was anxious to protect the USA's southern border, so he'd get started without the financial support he insisted would be forthcoming and take an IOU.

Only weeks after these statements were made, Mexican President Enrique Peña-Nieto cancelled a scheduled visit to Washington, DC, saying "Mexico does not believe in walls. I've said time and again – Mexico will not pay for any wall."

But at the heart of the Mexican President's cancellation was Trump's suggestion that Mexico's imports to the USA should be taxed at a rate of 20%.

This to one of the USA's top trading partners.

With the USA's relationship with its southern neighbor in tatters, Trump's MAGA slogan began to wear a little thin, just days after his Inauguration. There is nothing less "great" than publicly humiliating and attacking a primary trading partner.

But that trading partner was also the home of people Trump's most ardent and devoted supporters do not like – Mexicans. They dislike Mexicans to such a degree that they don't mind throwing a few billion US dollars at a wall to see if they stick; to see if building a wall (which needs to cross mountain ranges and cannot cross the Gulf of Mexico) will do the trick and stem the endless flow of "rapists and criminals" into US territories (most of which were gained in Guadalupe Hidalgo, courtesy of Mexico).

The defining slogan of the Trump campaign, MAGA, is an empty populist device to appeal to those who feel they've been left behind. Chief among them is the demographic which broke most overwhelmingly for Trump in the election – white males without college degrees.

This group sees itself as beleaguered by change. They no longer feel free to indulge in racial slurs or off-color jokes about women. They feel they've been left behind by a system which puts them last. For this disaffected group, the assertion that someone else must surely be to blame for their circumstances is an attractive one. It exonerates them from personal responsibility, placing the blame on an "other" which has taken their jobs and threatens their status as the face of the USA.

In all these assumptions is the most fertile ground for populism and the Trump campaign was painfully aware. Steve Bannon, the man who managed the Trump campaign and would later join his administration (and then, be summarily bounced out the door), deliberately exploited the aggrieved.

When you're able to convince a group of people which is angry and disaffected that there's someone to blame and that you know who it is, you can reflect back to it that anger. You're also able to give focus to the free-floating rage of having been lied to about what's rightfully yours.

Populism gives the enemy a face and a name. By distracting the target group with these divisive tactics, the door to plutocracy is thrown open and through it rushes a ruling elite. In the cabinet, or in the shadows, the swamp has not been drained. It has been topped up to overflowing.

And so, after a year in office, the USA finds itself in a state of turmoil. Divided and alienated from one another as we've ever been, our nation loses international traction every day. We lose the goodwill of neighbors and trading partners. We suffer repeated incidents of violence across the country. And these are not terrorist attacks perpetrated by ISIS. These are terrorist attacks perpetrated by fellow citizens – primarily white males.

If Trump is making American great again, then why are here? What have we gained?

Who is really benefiting from this presidency and of what does that benefit consist?

CHAPTER FOUR

THE SPUTNIK HAS LANDED

"Vladimir Putin himself directed the covert cyberattacks against our electoral system, against our democracy, apparently because he has a personal beef against me."

Hillary Clinton, December 2016

With the rise of former KGB intelligence officer to the most powerful role in the former Soviet Union, came a new order for the newly-reformed nation. It was an order ostensibly founded on Russian unity (as per the name of Vladimir Putin's political party, United Russia).

A politician forged in the "strong man" image so familiar in populism, Putin's old grudges against the United States were carried into office with him. Resentful of the ongoing projects of regime change practiced by George W. Bush, Putin held democracy and democratic movements in contempt.

But he developed an even more toxic grudge against the woman who would be the candidate for the Democratic Party in 2016 — Hillary

Rodham Clinton. It was in 2011, as Secretary of State under Obama, that Clinton would condemn the Russian parliamentary elections of the time.

These elections brought Russians into the streets of the nation's cities, protesting what they deemed to be a fraudulently achieved victory by Putin. Clinton's agreement with that characterization was seen by Putin as a threat to his own expansionist ambitions. He also blamed Clinton for Russia's domestic unrest.

Casting himself as next on the USA's perceived "hit list", Putin believed Clinton would become the next President and that he would meet the same fate Saddam Hussein had, in Iraq.

The Russians are here

In the spring of 2015, US intelligence intercepted conversations between officials of the Russian government. The subject of those conversations? Trump and his associates.

Following Trump's announcement of his candidacy in June of the following year, Twitter accounts began popping up, praising the candidate effusively. Many of these were fake accounts run out of the Kremlin by Russia's Internet Research Agency.

That summer, the Democratic National Committee's computers were hacked by the Federal Security Service of the Russian Federation. By doing so, the Russian government was able to deploy the information in the service of shifting the results of the 2016 presidential election.

Data was not only stolen from the DNC, though. It was also lifted from state and local jurisdictions and included information like partial social security numbers and data gleaned from driver's licenses, according to a June 22, 2017 article in TIME magazine. Thousands of voters were affected and at least one successful attempt to change voter information was made.

June 22 is the same date the House and Senate Intelligence committees convened and it was first acknowledged that interference in the elections by the Russians was much more extensive than originally believed.

It's been posited that Russian intelligence was able to breech security in all 50 states. Even if these incursions amounted only to "rattling the doorknob", as stated by Michael Daniel, charged with managing the interference by the Obama administration, voter confidence was shaken by these revelations.

While Robert Mueller continues to investigate the possibility of collusion between the Trump campaign and the Russian government (particularly its intelligence branch), there are some key factors which much be kept in mind when discussing that possibility.

The Sater connection

President Trump continues to insist that he doesn't even know who Felix Sater is. But there is abundant evidence to suggest he has had a relationship with him for many years.

Sater's claim to fame is as a Russian businessman with connections to organized crime. That status did not prevent him from being at the Trump campaign's victory party on election night. The election night gathering was invitation-only. Sater travelled from his home in Long Island by car service to attend the celebration, held at the Midtown Hilton.

But long before November 2016, Sater and Trump were well-acquainted with each other. In September 2007, he's pictured standing with Trump at the unveiling of the now beleaguered Trump SoHo.

A picture may be worth 1,000 words, but there are also words concerning the Trump/Sater relationship which bear repeating here. Here are some of the most important of them, relayed via email by Sater to Trump's lawyer, Andrew Cohen, on November 03, 2015.

"Our boy can become president of the USA and we can engineer it. I will get all of Putin's team to buy in on this, I will manage this process."

Early in the Trump campaign, operatives believed that forging close ties with Moscow would benefit the image of the candidate, casting him as a relationship-builder. But the very relationships being built are now being actively investigated by the US Justice Department and numerous congressional committees.

Part of Sater's plan to polish Trump's image as a dealmaker and the ideal candidate for

President, was to set up a deal with the Russian government, in which the Trump Organization would be able to build one of his famed golden towers in Russia.

To do this, Sater planned to set up financing with VTB Bank, a Russian banking entity under US sanctions for its role in undermining democratic elections in the Ukraine. (Also involved in those elections, of course, is Paul Manafort, instrumental in the Trump campaign and now under 12 indictments in the Mueller investigation, including charges of money laundering).

While none of Sater's promises concerning the Russian real estate deal were ever to come to fruition, he did make good on one promise.

Trump is now President.

RT and the trolls of misinformation
RT is the government-sponsored and run English language news agency at the center of allegations that the Russians actively worked to defame Hillary Clinton and praise Donald Trump, to deliver the US Presidency to him.

Vladimir Putin has stated that the agency was created in 2005 with a commission to break the

"Anglo-Saxon monopoly on the global information systems".

Available with some cable companies in the US, it can also be accessed online, so its reach in the USA is material and there is little question that RT played a pivotal role in the 2016 election.

In January 2017, the US Office of the Director of National Intelligence released a report confirming this. The report stated that RT was actively engaged in disseminating messaging favorable to the Russian government, as its mission. It also stated that programming on the network was clearly focused on "undermining viewers' trust of US democratic procedures".

And all this turned out to be a problem for Michael Flynn, formerly Trump's national security advisor. Flynn has appeared frequently on RT, but was also engaged by the news agency to attend a gala dinner celebrating its anniversary in 2015. He not only spoke at the event, but was seated next to Putin.

But Flynn had bigger problems than RT. He had also misled his colleagues about repeated contacts with Russian Ambassador to the US, Sergey Kislyak. This represented a profound breach of protocol, leaving Flynn vulnerable to blackmail. At issue were discussions with Kislyak, concerning US sanctions. While it has neither been proven nor disproven that these were discussed, the media had responded vociferously to the news of Flynn's lapses of judgment.

Flynn stepped down from his post in February.

Lies and hacking – cheaper than missiles

While its illustrious leader appears to be doing very well for himself, with a personal fortune veiled in mystery, numbered accounts and shell companies, Russia itself can't afford to compete with the USA and its allies in terms of weaponry. It's unable to challenge NATO, or the European Union, either.

Without the necessary financial resources to face down its ideological enemies, Putin has instead chosen a thrifty alternative – propaganda and hacking.

Lies come cheaper by the dozen and certainly cheaper than a dozen ICBMs.

All world democracies are in Putin's sites, from Sweden (who experienced the reach of his propaganda machine's tentacles when it voiced a plan to co-operate with NATO militarily), to the Ukraine.

During the Ukrainian presidential elections of 2014, it's been demonstrated that Russia interfered directly by attempting to manipulate vote totals. Joseph Kiniry, who is a cyber-security professional in the realm of voting systems, told the Christian Science Monitor that this was the first instance of a foreign attempt to influence the outcome of elections in a democratic nation ever witnessed on such a vast scale.

But it was not to be the only one, by any means.

Bulgaria, Austria, Norway, the Netherlands, France and the UK have all seen similar incursions dedicated to manipulating election results.

Candidate Trump even went so far as to invite Russia to interfere, when he called on the Federation to "find the 30,000 (of candidate Clinton's) emails that are missing", on July 27, 2016.

The WikiLeaks connection

In every presidential election, the October Surprise is information held in abeyance until a critical point in the election cycle is reached. This information has the power to sway undecided voters with (usually) explosive revelations which clinch their support for one candidate or the other.

October 2016 was no exception. Out of a clear blue sky, WikiLeaks revealed to the media that it was in possession of emails from Clinton campaign chair, John Podesta. At the time, intelligence officials declared that WikiLeaks was being used as a conduit to syphon information unfavorable to the Clinton campaign to news agencies.

Surprise.

The Director of National Intelligence and the Department of Homeland Security pull no punches in their condemnation of Russian involvement, clearly implicating the Russian government with the release of the emails.

Podesta was also unequivocal in his indictment of the Russians, saying, "This level of meddling by a foreign power can only be aimed at boosting Donald Trump and should send chills down the spine of all Americans, regardless of political party."

For his part, shadowy figure Julian Assange (founder and editor of WikiLeaks), denied any involvement by the Russians. Currently taking refuge in the Ecuadorian Embassy in London, from rape charges leveled against him in Sweden, Assange is now recognized as being a central facilitator of the Russians, particularly in the release of emails and WikiLeaks' role as a conduit for that purpose.

Since its first sally into the media spotlight in 2010, WikiLeaks has consistently devoted itself to leaking information which is embarrassing to the USA and its allies. This drew him to the attention of Vladimir Putin.

Assange's relationship with Putin and his administration began in April 2012, when Assange became a regular presence on RT. He was given his own show, called "The World Tomorrow", playing the role of host. In so doing, he was paid by the progenitor of RT, itself – the Kremlin.

Assange is also credited with facilitating Edward Snowden's departure to Russia, to elude charges against him under the US Espionage Act, due to his leaking of over 1 million documents, the bulk of which directly concerned (and threatened) US intelligence and military operations.

Clearly, Assange's denials of Russian involvement in the October Surprise email dump are hollow. His involvement with Putin and the Russian state are of long standing and the character of his efforts toward "transparency" at WikiLeaks have routinely undermined the United States of America.

But there is one instance we should take special note of here. On October 7, the Washington Post released audio provided by Access Hollywood of candidate Trump's infamous remarks about grabbing women by their private parts. Only one hour after this release, WikiLeaks released the Podesta emails.

48 hours of breathless coverage of the emails (which contained little of interest) later and the deleterious impact of Trump's misogynist bragging was blunted.

In the words of candidate Clinton, "WikiLeaks is unfortunately now practically a fully owned subsidiary of Russian intelligence."

To kill a democracy

It's clear that Vladimir Putin is not a huge fan of democracy. Russia, under his leadership, has become a place in which the leader is to be praised. Journalists, diplomats and conscientious objectors to his manner of governing are summarily punished. Some get jail time. Others disappear.

But what's also clear is that Vladimir Putin's longstanding grudge against a Secretary of State who took the side of Russian protestors against him is a key factor in his intense interest in the US election of 2016.

Using complex modes of interference, including the theft and subsequent deployment of information, Russia not only achieved a public distrust of traditional and well-respected media outlets (echoed by Trump, himself), it achieved a public distrust of democracy itself.

Worse still, it created a distrust of neighbor. Americans are now at odds with one another in a way they haven't been for decades. We are divided into camps as surely as we were during the Civil War and the Civil Rights Era.

And all around us, there is evidence that our nation is fracturing.

In the next chapter, we'll examine the motivations of Donald Trump in seeking the Office of the President. We'll also examine why he became the Trojan horse of a quasi-dictator, and the forces which surround him in the biggest mafia state in the world, intent on the destruction of the USA and democracy, itself.

CHAPTER 5

THE TROJAN HORSE

Born to wealth and privilege, Donald Trump has always been known as a flamboyant figure. Presenting an almost cartoonish persona, what he's most famous for is his reputation as a wheeling, dealing businessman.

That reputation was spun into a larger than life host of now defunct reality show, The Apprentice. But Trump has also made numerous cameo appearances in a variety of films, appeared in television advertisements and rather oddly, on many episodes of the WWE'S WrestleMania wrestling spectacles.

Donald Trump likes to be the center of attention.

Unlike many businessmen, he's made it a mission to remain in the eye of any hurricane passing by, throwing himself into the whirlwind at the slightest provocation.

What could be more enticing than the role of the most powerful leader in the world — President of the USA, for one so enamored of the spotlight? The light shines on you all day, every day.

If you sneeze, it's news.

Trump's longstanding reputation as a larger-than-life figure is mostly attributable to his own branding efforts. The brand is not a hotel, or a casino. It's not steaks or wine. It's him. He is the brand. The grand swoop of his hair serves as a logo, as well as his signature irascibility and tendency to take the smallest slight as a searing affront.

As we've read earlier, it's clear that Vladimir Putin desired Trump's presence in the Oval Office. Putin's machinations and those of his army of hackers and trolls created conditions whereby it was possible for Donald Trump – a person of uneven disposition, a business career checkered by failure and ambiguous political affiliations – to become President.

But why? What did the Russian Federation have to gain by ensuring he rose to this position?

The plasticity of narcissism
Surely, Putin knew that the project would come with an incredible amount of risk. A man as

well-acquainted with the engines of power as Putin is, went into the affair with eyes fully opened. He was willing to interfere with an American election and suffer the consequences. And why was that so desperately important to him?

As the Mueller investigation closes in, revelations about contact between Donald Trump Jr. and a Russian government lawyer have muddied the waters even further.

Sought by Trump in the meeting (which he denied even attending) was information about former Secretary of State Clinton which might prove damaging to her campaign. Also in attendance were the President's son-in-law, Jared Kushner and the now indicted Paul Manafort, Trump campaign Chair.

Where did Putin's interest come from?

Historically Trump, his family and business associates have enjoyed a cordial relationship with Russia, its government and its business interests – oligarchs included. But that still doesn't answer the question.

Why?

Was Putin so anxious to exact vengeance on Hillary Clinton that he was willing to do everything in his power to prevent her from becoming President? Was he being eaten up with existential angst about the prospect of going the way of Saddam Hussein?

But under intense media scrutiny in July 2017, Trump was to claim that Putin's preference had been Clinton. Making vague claims concerning Putin's approval of the job he'd being doing as President to that point, he told Pat Robertson in an interview for the Christian Broadcast Corporation, that he did "many things that are the exact opposite of what he (Putin) would want".

Unfortunately for Trump, this claim meant very little in the glare of media attention, directed to the possibility that his administration had possibly colluded with Russia to win the White House. No one was buying it, save the diehard base.

Or was there another purpose in Putin's mind, in choosing this mercurial, extravagantly ungovernable personality to be his Trojan horse? Did he perhaps see in him a malleability, governed by Trump's obsession with fame, ratings and public exposure?

Did he know something about Donald Trump that others didn't? The Steele dossier (with its tales of Russian prostitutes and urination) may hold the key. What's more likely is that Trump's business ventures in Russia tell at least part of the story.

While Russian sanctions have been rumored to have been put on the table by the Trump administration, what's interesting to note here is the long term (and disturbing) relationship with a nation the USA was once locked in a prolonged Cold War for world primacy with.

We've already discussed Trump's relationship with Felix Sater, but the Russian connections don't end there. Trump also has ties to Bayrock Associates, of which Sater was managing director.

Bayrock, subject of a 2015 anti-racketeering case, has been described as "mob-owned and operated". In the case, Trump's SoHo development is cited as a sterling example of the corruption of this company. The development itself stood as a monument to "money laundering and tax evasion".

And yet, Trump collaborated with this company on the Fort Lauderdale Trump Tower, the SoHo development noted above and two other projects in the USA.

All four of these projects eventually failed.

But it's Trump's visit to Russia in 2013 that's probably the most damning of all his tangled connections to that nation. Staying in Russia during the Miss Universe pageant, it's during this time that Trump met with a series of Russian businessmen directly embroiled with Putin. This has been confirmed by Herman Gref, CEO of Sherbank, a state-controlled Russian bank sanctioned by the both the European Union and the USA for its involvement in Russia's invasion of the Ukraine in 2014.

As late as the opening months 2017, Felix Sater again emerges as a close ally of Trump. Only a week before Michael Flynn's departure from the Trump cadre, three Russians visited the White House. They bore with them a proposal for the elimination of Russian sanctions. Those men?

Andrew Cohen, Trump's personal lawyer, AndriiArtemenko, a Ukrainian parlimentarian on the side of the Russians and Felix Sater.

Why Sater, already convicted of fraud and implicated in money-laundering and other crimes by virtue of his position with Bayrock, would be implicated in such high-level discussions, is a matter for careful consideration.

He is neither an elected official nor a diplomatic representative of the Russian Federation, so the question is one which should make the hairs on the back of your neck stand up.

And the GOP, the party presiding over the elimination of the Berlin Wall and the subsequent dismantling of the former Soviet Union, seems all too willing to go along with whatever mischief this unpredictable occupant of the White House gets up to. It routinely and deliberately excuses his actions with a reductionism which must surely require a set of blinkers to be maintained.

Trumpian chaos.

Donald Trump is known to be a disruptive influence in every sector he occupies. In business, he is known to have declared bankruptcy in his Atlantic City casino operations on three different occasions. As a candidate for President, his rallies were typified by violence, dog whistle politics to inflame his supporters and tremendous errors in judgement concerning his comportment that kept news media buzzing about his fitness for the role, throughout the cycle.

The Trump presidency is no departure from this theme. In Executive Order after Executive Order, the President has deliberately set out to undo all the work of the previous administration. Meanwhile, Congress pounds away at undoing the work of the past 60 years of progress and the building of a just society, as Trumps golfs, tweets and rampages on his international visits like a bull in a china shop.

Is chaos in the heart of the greatest world power of the 20th and thus far, 21st Centuries, at the heart of Putin's ambitions? Does he desire all semblance of ordered governance to be destroyed, to weaken the USA – to demoralize and divide its people to an even greater degree than it's already become?

Perhaps. The moral authority of the US as a world power is certainly eroded when the nation he leads is in disarray, its executive branch sparsely staffed, with power coalescing around the President and a small cadre in his administration, including members of his own family. It's that moral authority which has buoyed up international solidarity around the missions of our country and cemented our relationships with allies.

But it is rapidly eroding. When the President of the United States continues to support a candidate for Senate who is has been accused by numerous women of sexual harassment while they were in their teens, moral chaos has descended. The truculence of the President in this instance is only one of many indications that he is completely unconcerned with the gravitas of the office he now holds. Further, that he cleaves to a belief in party loyalty which transcends the wellbeing of American citizens, especially the women complaining against Roy Moore's serial misbehaviors, is unprecedented in modern American history.

Most Presidents would have rescinded their support. But not Trump. Trump doubles down when he's in a politically dangerous position, a tendency seen repeatedly since his Inauguration.

Decades of debt

In a 2008 interview, Donald Trump Jr. said the Trump Organization saw "a lot of money pouring in from Russia", further stating that this money represented the bulk of the organization's assets at the time.

SevaGunitsky is a University of Toronto politics professor who's been following the Trump/Russia money chain for a decade. In a recent interview with online publication Vox, he provided key insight into the extent of Trump's Russian money funnel.

The interview touches on a crucial element of this funnel in the death of Sergei Magnitsky in a Russian prison, in 2009. Magnitsky was a Russian tax accountant actively investigating fraud practiced by officials of the Russian tax agency.

The Magnitsky Act, a bi-partisan bill passed in 2012, sought to punish those responsible in the

Russian government they believed were responsible for Magnitsky's beating death in prison. The legislation effectively barred these officials from entering the USA and prohibited them from the use of US banks.

The Prevezon case was the result of Magnitsy's investigations into a massive fraud scheme he'd unearthed in 2008. It was these investigations which led to his imprisonment and death. A case being mounted against Prevezon by the US Attorney was abruptly and mysteriously dropped.

According to the Gunitsky interview, the case was immediately dropped upon the ascension to office of Donald Trump. The case, which had been painstakingly prepared and was ready to proceed, was suddenly settled and for a shockingly low amount - $6 million.

Right before the case was dropped and the settlement was reached. PreetBharara, the attorney leading the case, was fired from his position as US Attorney for the Southern District of New York.

So, it seems there's more to the Trojan horse's entry to the White House than political intrigue. There is a great deal of money involved and in money, there is leverage. Prevezon, it's also widely known, laundered massive amounts of money via New York real estate transactions on behalf of shadowy interests. When this factor is considered against recent revelations concerning Trump's property in Panama and the money laundering which has been associated with that property, a strong theme begins to emerge.

At work here, is a love of money so powerful, that all other interests pale in significance. Clearly, there are strong connections between Trump and Russian financial interests (some of which bear the indelible stamp of criminality). Notably, political interests being driven by the promise of inestimable financial gain may be nothing new, but the role of money in the Trump/Russia connection is of such huge importance that it may, indeed, be driving the foreign policy of our nation.

And that is a tremendous threat to national security.

Trump's relationship with Russian oligarchs, especially, is concerning. What does he owe them and are these debts, accumulated over decades, providing the Russian Federation with political leverage, even to the point of collusion in elections?

Is Donald Trump so indebted to the Russians that he was never in any position to defend the interests of the United States over his own?

Inside the gates

For 17 years, Vladimir Putin has ruled over the former Soviet Union. During that time, he has amassed a fortune. Nobody appears able to discern its magnitude. Like Trump, his financial status is murky and mysterious.

Like Trump, he does not release his tax returns.

The post-Soviet incarnation of Russia is a place in which the lines between political power and financial power are blurred into insignificance. The two worlds overlap and meld.

And now, the same may be said of the USA. With his extensive and longstanding financial ties to Russia, the President is essentially indebted to both governmental and criminal partners. By his son's own admission, much of the financial health of the Trump Organization by be traced to Russian sources.

There are, for example, at least 13 known individuals (most with criminal connections) who have owned, leased and run illegal operations out of Trump's properties for over 3 decades. The roots run deep and the debt is yet unknown.

After having repeatedly pushed his business empire to the brink of ruin, Russia has been a salvific force in Trump's professional life, infusing it with needed cash. That cash is what propelled Trump into the spotlight of television and later, politics.

What's becoming clear, upon examination of these connections, is that the oligarchs of Russia saw in Trump a malleable buffoon; someone they could easily and readily manipulate. While it's unclear how much Trump knew about the criminality of some of his benefactors, what is clear is that he is deeply indebted to them.

Described by Boris Yeltson as "the biggest mafia state in the world", the Russia which would emerge from the collapse of the Soviet Union, was one in which rapidly amassed fortunes could be made overnight.

It's estimated that since that time, $1.3 trillion dollars in capital generated by organized crime has oozed out of Russia. Millions of dollars of that was directed at Trump's casinos and luxury real estate developments, particularly casinos in Atlantic City.

During the 1990s, Trump's serial failures at business would result in multiple declarations of bankruptcy. Owing $4 billion to over 70 different banks, he scrambled to stay afloat. But Russia's default on its own debt, in 1998, would cause these two flagging worlds to collide.

The Russian mafia was anxious to protect its assets, seeking safe havens for its money. In October of 1998, Trump would turn the soil for the famed Trump Tower in Manhattan. Two-thirds of available units were rapidly bought by interests from Russia, the Ukraine and Kazakhstan.

This pattern repeated through the era at other Trump properties. The Russian mafia had found a safe and reliable hiding place for its loot. At his Florida property alone, these interests are responsible for a whopping $98 million in revenue.

And what had Donald Trump found? Resurrection in the public consciousness, following a string of failures and missteps which brought him to the brink of catastrophe. With the influx of Russian cash, he was not only able to recuperate, he was able to launch himself into a lucrative television career (having been paid $3 million per episode for The Apprentice) and finally, to ascend to the role of President.

No spotlight has ever been more pleasing to him. No spotlight has ever been more revelatory of the true source of his wealth. No spotlight has ever revealed a more abject snapshot of foreign influence and corruption.

Now inside our gates, the Trojan horse has broken through all measures to secure the interests of our country. And Putin is just the tip of the iceberg. The Biggest Mafia State in the World now holds in its hands a President with little knowledge of the mechanics or government and little interest in them.

Trump's interests are not ideological. He is uniquely detached from anything resembling an ideology, having been (variously) a Reform Party candidate, a supporter of the Democratic

Party, a Republican Party candidate for nominee and now, a Republican President.

Trump's purpose, whether he's aware of it or not, is the Trojan horse by which an army of oligarchs and international criminals has leaped from its belly, inside the gates. Whether unwitting dupe, or collaborator, Trump has, by his own hand, invited destabilizing forces into the precincts of the White House, where there is influence, even greater riches and a conduit to all they desire, in the person of the President.

As we stand divided, wondering where all the winning we were promised during the campaign has gone to, Robert Mueller mounts his case, handing down indictments and throwing the entire administration's validity into profound doubt.

Civil War is being threatened. A motion to Impeach has been made. And Putin smiles from the Kremlin, as the USA groans under the weight of a scandal which promises to make Watergate look like a kid shoplifting Lifesavers.

Where do we go from here?

With competing voices pulling our attention from one side of the argument to the other, many Americans are confused. Who to believe? What to think?

And there is only one answer to the chaos and confusion rising all around us. Engagement. Engaging with every possible source of information available to make connections and to unveil the truth, is the responsibility of every American, right now.

As we have in the past, we can again unite behind a shared idea of the USA as a moral authority and world leader. It doesn't matter if we're Republicans, Democrats, Independents, or even Greens. What matters most urgently is that we're Americans and what we've just collectively experienced is nothing short of a foreign invasion by a hostile power.

If we are who we say we are and we treasure our democratic institutions and their role in making us an international exemplar of democracy, then we are duty bound to demand answers concerning Donald Trump and the channels by which he ascended to the Presidency.

As the Mueller investigation continues, it's helpful to remember that Watergate took no less than 900 days to compel the resignation of Richard M. Nixon. Seen in those terms, Mueller is a young enterprise, yet to provide its most damning evidence.

While it's easy to choose less complicated matters to hang our outrage on (the reversals of Barack Obama's ban on the importation of elephant tusks, for one), Russia is what genuinely and most vociferously demands our attention. To not understand the presenting issue here – the sovereignty and security of our nation – is to stand unarmed on a field populated by forces who are armed to the teeth.

Where we go from here is from a place of quiet horror and numbness, to one of full engagement. We are citizens before we are taxpayers. We are Americans before we are members of a political party, or of any ethnicity, or a religion.

And unless my historical recall is sorely lacking, I seem to remember a time when Americans stood up to enemies (either domestic or foreign), with resolve and determination, as a unified group.

The unquenchable flame that lives in every American heart still burns. It needs to burn brighter and burn in unity. It needs to burn so bright that it consumes all that stands between us and the truth about Russia's involvement in the Trump Organization and the 2016 presidential election.

We are Americans. We must be united to stem the tide of chaos in our nation and we must demand that the truth, in its entirety, be told. We are not a nation of spectators. We are a nation of active participants who work together to find the way forward for our country and its people.

The chaos is temporary. Certainly, our history instructs that this is so. All the same, if we're to turn its tide, our personal accountability needs to be reborn in us. We must vote. To vote intelligently, we must be informed. Between elections, we must engage at every level of government, questioning all we hear and see and always demanding that those we elect never forget who their boss is.

We are.

We are the USA, in all its diversity. E Pluribus Unum is our battle cry. It's we who have the power to Make America Great Again, lifting up the former devastations as a nation united in its commitment to be a beacon of democracy and justice, around the world.

CONCLUSION

The Buddhist greeting "Namaste" is instructive in our current quest to restore unity, American to American.

Meaning "the light in me acknowledges the light in you," the greeting takes explicit note of the presence of God in other creatures. The spirit of Namaste brings people closer together by recognizing the common bond we all have through our Creator.

By whatever name we know God, in the context of whatever religious system we espouse, there is only one God and we are all brothers and sisters in that Divine reality.

The USA is one of the most diverse nations on earth. In that truth is both challenge and opportunity. Diversity offers a type of strength not available in societies which don't permit for it, or haven't fostered it.

Diversity offers us the unique worldviews of disparate groups and the experiences those worldviews have been developed from. There's a reason for the continual innovation and the forging of paths others haven't forged, emanating from our nation.

And that reason is not conformity of thought. From the foundation of our nation, there has been significant divergence. We are not a nation of conformity. We are a nation in which the primacy of the individual is paramount; in which each of us has value and something unique to offer.

But it's often the case that our very diversity leads certain segments of our population to claim themselves as the only "true" or "real" Americans. Eruptions of this effect can be seen throughout our history, but manifestations which reject diversity continue to this day.

Torch-bearing white supremacists and militias in fatigues, festooned with guns, march in our streets. Their numbers, while dwarfed by those who oppose their retreat to tribalism, are alarming, when it's considered that this faction is more likely to own multiple weapons than any other group.

Most of us see the light in one another. In each other's eyes, we can see the unquenchable flame flicker in defiance of all that divides us as

Americans. But the advent of Donald Trump has quickened the moribund minority, emboldening it to step again into the public square.

And this time, they've left their white hoods at home.

And in that tribalism is yet another challenge to our continuing health and possibly the continuing existence of our Union. Simmering resentments, far from being soothed by the steady hand of a leader, are being fanned by hands seeking to divide us further.

In a democratic society, it's incumbent on the people to attend to governmental matters as a function of citizenship.

This fact has never been more potently clear.

As we've slept, mouthing excuses for our disengagement like, "They're all the same" and "I don't care about politics", a rot has set in around our national democratic institutions. The oligarchs of Russia and their figurehead, Vladimir Putin, are aware of this effect. It represents a gap between our stated values and beliefs and reality.

And it's through that gap that those who seek to bring down a world power slither. It's through that gap, that the degradation of our democratic institutions is sought by those who would most richly benefit from the loss of international moral authority.

It's through that gap that organized crime and its facilitators have gained the Office of the White House, occupied by a Trojan horse who may or may not know his purpose in the hands of Putin and his operatives.

With the Mueller investigation continuing apace, we stand on the brink of either disaster or renaissance. Much of what happens next depends on our commitment to our nation, but also, our commitment to our neighbor.

The American vision of brotherhood and common purpose is all that stands between us and the chaos engulfing our nation. If we believe what we say – if it matters to us that this great experiment be vindicated by history – then we are all enjoined to be the citizens we are, as Americans.

It's in our citizenship that the seeds of renewal lie and it's in our connection to one another, as

Americans united in common purpose, that victory over the forces seeking to tear our beloved nation apart is found.

We are the wall which stands between who we say we are and who others desire us to be. We will not serve a foreign master. We will serve the dream of freedom, liberty and justice for all for that is the legacy of the American people.

Awake and engaged, we will demand and work together for the vision of America we all believe in – a united America in which the unquenchable flame is raised aloft in the service of decency and in the spirit of courage. The statue of Liberty is not made of flesh and blood. We are.

We now know that they are not "all the same".

We have now seen why we must care about politics.

Our commission to this nation is clear.

Citizens, light the fire in your hearts and reclaim what is rightfully yours – the dream of the United States of America.It doesn't matter whether you believe Donald J. Trump to be a racist himself. What matters is that his campaign rhetoric has ignited not the unquenchable flame of American kinship, but the raging inferno of tribalist bigotry.

Unhinged from the decorum of his office and tethered to the interests of the Russian Federation and its oligarchs, so lavishly fed by organized crime, we have in the White House a Trojan horse.

Whether a knowing collaborator, or an unwitting tool, Donald Trump is the pore through which the virus has entered the host, corrupting and sickening it – driving it to its knees. Whether selling himself to Pilate for 30 pieces of silver – a deal with the Devil to gain the powerful Office in the world – or not, Donald Trump's status as debtor to forces beyond our borders is the problematic reality.

And it's that reality we're ultimately left with.

www.ingramcontent.com/pod-product-compliance
Lightning Source LLC
Chambersburg PA
CBHW051827250726
48659CB00005B/1716